Managing

Information

YOUR SELF-
DEVELOPMENT
ACTION PLAN

PETER GRAINGER

 **NP**

Kogan Page Ltd, London
Nichols Publishing Company,
New Jersey

First published in 1994

Apart from any fair dealing for the purposes of research or
private study, or criticism, as permitted under the Copyright,
Designs and Patents Act, 1988, this publication may only be
reproduced, stored or transmitted, in any form or by any means,
with the prior permission in writing of the publishers, or in the
case of reprographic reproduction in accordance with the terms of
licences issued by the Copyright Licensing Agency. Enquiries
concerning reproduction outside those terms should be sent to the
publishers at the undermentioned address:

Kogan Page Limited
120 Pentonville Road
London N1 9JN

© Peter Grainger, 1994

Published in the United States of America by Nichols Publishing,
PO Box 6036, East Brunswick, New Jersey 08816

British Library Cataloguing in Publication Data

A CIP record for this book is available from the British Library.

ISBN (UK) 0 7494 1248 8
ISBN (US) 0-89397-432-3

Typeset by the author
Printed and bound in Great Britain by Biddles Ltd, Guildford and
King's Lynn.

CONTENTS

PREFACE

It has taken more than 20 years to refine the 12 generic skills of management, which are the foundation of the Manager's Toolkit series, into a form which is both straightforward enough for busy managers to learn and which actually works in real life.

The skills contained in the original *Manager's Toolkit* manual and the linked style definitions were developed in the course of 15 years' management experience in senior training and development positions with Rank Xerox. Unique opportunities existed in the company at that time for creative approaches to the training and development of first-level and middle managers on both sides of the Atlantic.

As a member of a number of specialist teams in the USA and Europe, I was fortunate to come into personal contact with many of the most effective management techniques of recent times – for example, the systematic approach of Charles Kepner and Ben Tregoe and the Huthwaite Research Group's 'Interactive Skills'.

The first step was to build these techniques into a set of 'Management Standards' which the management teams of Rank Xerox's manufacturing plants in the UK developed over a number of years, and then test them in *practical* situations, including residential training programmes.

Every manager participating in a training programme brought a real-life problem to the course, and the skills taught were applied to each of those 'issues' during the programme. If a technique did not work or took too long to apply, it was discarded or modified.

After ten years of running intensive management development programmes at all levels, we had so refined the techniques that they could be integrated into a comprehensive 'toolkit' of skills that would actually guarantee results (pages 10–12).

At this time, my later business partner, Roger Acland, and I developed the personal style definitions which became an essential ingredient of all our work, and from which I later created the 'Personal Development Toolkit' and the Style Profile (page 37).

This integrated learning approach, built upon the need for positive thinking (page 26), has proved its special value to groups of managers and potential managers drawn from a wide range of organizations, from students, accountants, and engineers to teams in Allied Lyons, Rank Xerox and British Telecom.

The great benefit of the approach is that it is quick to use, flexible – *and it works*. After years of practical application, the 12 skills have now been honed to such simple effectiveness that they can be readily acquired through open learning. Look through the structure and methodology of the book to see how the approach works in practice for the three 'Information' skills contained in this manual.

I believe the hundreds of organizations of all sizes that have purchased the original *Manager's Toolkit* manual since its publication in 1992 provide ample confirmation of the simple effectiveness of both the content and the method of learning.

Peter Grainger

INTRODUCTION

INTRODUCTION

1. The approach

The Manager's Toolkit series is designed to be suitable for a wide range of managers. You may already be a manager responsible for the work of other people and want to learn how to make more of yourself and the resources under your control. You may be facing the prospect of the responsibility of managing – or you may want to take an opportunity to manage when it arises – and be uncertain how to set about it.

To make the most of the books in the series you will either not have received any management training or the training you have received will have only given you *knowledge* of management and not the practical skills of *how* to manage.

Statistics show that few managers have received any formal training. I suspect most managers are too busy – or too exhausted – to find time to study 'management' literature. The style of each book in the series is therefore as economical and as visual as possible, concentrating on making clear each step of each process or skill – more like a DIY car manual than a learned business treatise.

The series will not only explain the essential generic skills of managing yourself and others but will give you opportunities to *practise* those skills as you apply them to your own real-life situations. The comprehensive Index on pages 95 and 96 provides you with easy access when you have a specific skills need.

In addition to acquiring such essential skills as specifying targets and standards and chairing meetings, you will come to understand yourself better, the person behind the manager or potential manager.

Some people master some of the skills of management more readily than others because of the sort of *person* they are. Some people are good with information but not with people, others are good with people but poor at taking action.

You will analyse your *personal style* in relation to three style definitions and as a result determine which are the most important skills for you personally to work on (see pages 38–9). You can therefore create your own development plan from the moment you buy the first book, confident that you are using your learning time most effectively.

Finally, you will gradually build up a *positive approach* to the situations in which you find yourself as a manager. Developing positive expectations of people and situations is a critical part of leadership and management. It has to be acquired and continuously worked at. It is not just a matter of attitude, but of applying particular techniques. Anyone can learn these techniques and so make a remarkable difference not only to the way they manage but also to the impact they make on the world about them.

2. The toolkit of skills

The Manager's Toolkit series consists of four personal development workbooks designed as open learning training and development aids to enable anyone who wants to be able to manage – or manage better – to acquire the necessary skills in their own time and at their own pace.

The series is based on the single volume *The Manager's Toolkit*, which I published in 1992, and was bought by large numbers of human resource specialists in large and small organizations throughout the United Kingdom. It was felt that making the *Toolkit* available *as a series* in a smaller format at lower cost would bring it within reach of individual managers and potential managers as and when they required each group of skills.

The concept of an *integrated* 'toolkit' of skills provides you with the opportunity to use the skills in sequence (for example in a major project), or skill-by-skill according to your personal need.

The formation of the toolkit shown opposite was the basis of the original *Manager's Toolkit*. The 12 key skills emerged from more complex models, and in numerical sequence represent a sequential, cyclical *process of management*, from clarifying roles (1) to giving and receiving feedback (12).

Each skill is not only important in its own right, but also links with its neighbours in making up *clusters* of skills for particular purposes, for example in this model to provide a

The Toolkit of Skills
a process of management

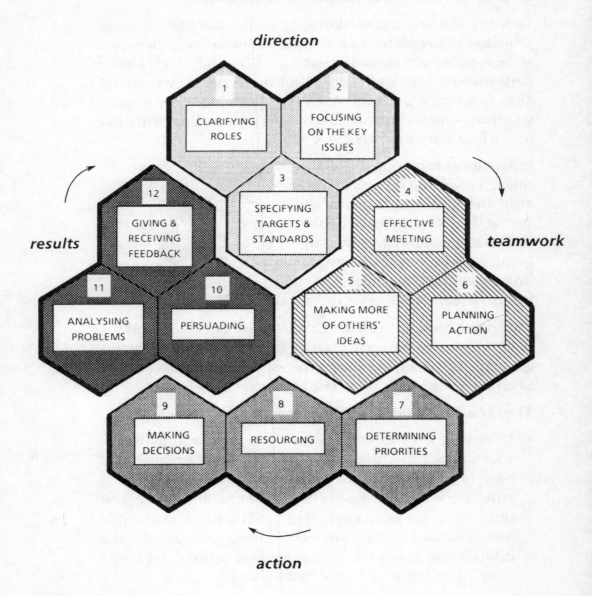

direction

1 CLARIFYING ROLES

2 FOCUSING ON THE KEY ISSUES

3 SPECIFYING TARGETS & STANDARDS

12 GIVING & RECEIVING FEEDBACK

4 EFFECTIVE MEETING

results

teamwork

11 ANALYSIING PROBLEMS

10 PERSUADING

5 MAKING MORE OF OTHERS' IDEAS

6 PLANNING ACTION

9 MAKING DECISIONS

8 RESOURCING

7 DETERMINING PRIORITIES

action

© *PETER GRAINGER 1994*

sense of *direction*, to make the most of a group, ie *teamwork*, to make things happen, ie *action*, or to make sure you do actually get the *results* you set out to achieve.

To bring the original toolkit of 12 skills into line with the priorities of the Management Charter Initiative's 'elements of competence', 'communicating' (7) and 'developing performance' (11) were added and the skills they replaced absorbed into associated skills (see page 11). The overall structure (opposite) was then brought into line with the MCI's four-part 'key roles' (see page 17).

With the *operations* skills of 'clarifying roles', 'specifying targets and stand-ards' and 'planning action' at the core of the toolkit, the particular skills associated with managing *people*, *resources* and *information* link conveniently with each of them to form a toolkit model for the series.

Each workbook in the series explores three essential skills in depth, providing opportunities for *open learning* practice at each step of the learning process. The process, common to all the workbooks, is explained on pages 20–1.

The three 'information' skills covered by this volume are:

- **Focusing on the key issues** (2) is a process by which you sort out the information relating to a problem you have to resolve or a task you have to complete. It is most valuable when the issue is large and unmanageable, and the information you are trying to handle is considerable and confused. The process enables you to get the information into units of manageable action, and so set your priorities with a clear perspective.

The Manager's Toolkit Series

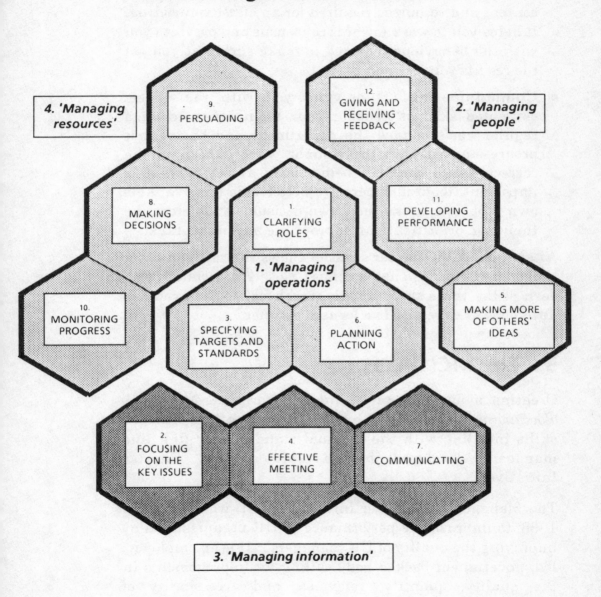

4. 'Managing resources'

9. PERSUADING

12. GIVING AND RECEIVING FEEDBACK

2. 'Managing people'

8. MAKING DECISIONS

1. CLARIFYING ROLES

11. DEVELOPING PERFORMANCE

1. 'Managing operations'

10. MONITORING PROGRESS

3. SPECIFYING TARGETS AND STANDARDS

6. PLANNING ACTION

5. MAKING MORE OF OTHERS' IDEAS

2. FOCUSING ON THE KEY ISSUES

4. EFFECTIVE MEETING

7. COMMUNICATING

3. 'Managing information'

- **Effective meeting** (4) enables you to plan the purpose, content and resources required for an effective meeting. It helps you to work towards consensus and provides you with the behaviour required to make sure that you get the results you planned.

- **Communicating** (7) provides you with the under-estimated skill of keeping your team informed on a regular basis of how the department and business is progressing, so that individuals' work is seen in the correct perspective. In being made aware of what is important, team members are better able to solve their own problems, make their own decisions and determine their own priorities in an appropriate business context.

After each skills chapter a model shows the skills in other books in the series that are most closely associated with each of the three skills in this workbook, so that you can develop your expertise in a focused manner.

3. The MCI links

Creating a four-part series from the original *Manager's Toolkit* manual provided an opportunity to bring the 12 skills into line with the national standards for first line managers developed by the Management Charter Initiative.

The Management Charter Initiative (MCI) was formed in 1988 'to improve the performance of UK organisations by improving the quality of UK managers'. It is an employer-led, government-backed body calling for improvements in the quality, quantity, relevance and accessibility of management education and development.

After extensive consultation, research and testing, the MCI is establishing a framework of four levels for management and supervisory development (Supervisory, Certificate, Diploma and Masters), with assessments based on demonstrated ability to manage. The guidelines at each of these levels give clear guidance on what is expected of managers at different levels, providing specific requirements for their development and assessment.

Detailed standards have been established for Supervisors, First Level Managers and Middle Managers, and I have taken the *First Level Management Standards* as the most appropriate link to the skills in the Manager's Toolkit series. They provide the management reference point for the National Vocational Qualifications at Level 4.

The standards first break down the key *roles* of management into first *units* and then *elements of competence*. Those covered in this workbook are:

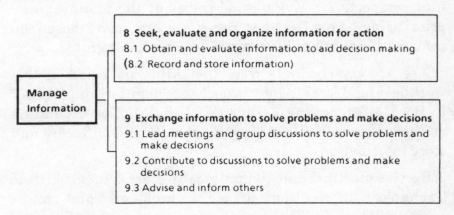

'Manage finance' has been broadened into *Managing Resources* to cover *all* resources, and includes 'making decisions', a skill essential to managing resources, and especially to 'contribute to the recruitment and selection of personnel' (*Unit 4, opposite*).

The first three elements of Unit 6 – '*plan, allocate...work*' – have been included in the 'operations' workbook because they link effectively with clarifying roles, tasks and plans.

As a result, a number of references in Element 6.4 (eg 'organizational guidelines' and 'systems/procedures') link directly with the skills in that workbook, rather than the skills in 'Managing People'.

In this workbook 'obtaining and evaluating information' (8.1) is covered by the use of the process of identifying 'help' and 'hinder' factors as an aid to getting a problem or task into perspective. 'Evaluation' comes at the planning and prioritising stage, so that decisions are made based on information that has been sorted into a meaningful shape.

There are clearly links from the skills contained in this workbook and 'making decisions' and 'monitoring progress' in Book 4, 'Managing Resources'. I shall not be expanding on the less specifically management skills in 8.2, 'record and store information'.

'Effective meeting' and 'communicating' are critical skills to 'exchange information to solve problems and make decisions' (Unit 9). This *exchange* not only involves 'leading' and 'contributing' to 'group discussions', but also 'advising and informing' (9.3). An explanation of the structure of 'interpersonal skills' which underlie these skills follows.

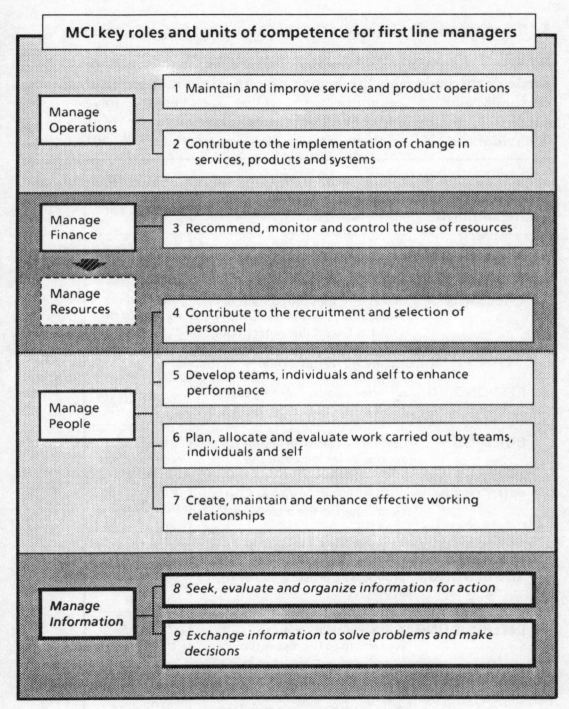

MCI key roles and units of competence for first line managers

Manage Operations
1 Maintain and improve service and product operations

2 Contribute to the implementation of change in services, products and systems

Manage Finance
3 Recommend, monitor and control the use of resources

Manage Resources
4 Contribute to the recruitment and selection of personnel

Manage People
5 Develop teams, individuals and self to enhance performance

6 Plan, allocate and evaluate work carried out by teams, individuals and self

7 Create, maintain and enhance effective working relationships

Manage Information
8 Seek, evaluate and organize information for action

9 Exchange information to solve problems and make decisions

4. Interpersonal Skills

In this 'Managing Information' workbook we shall be particularly concerned with managing *verbal* information, eg at meetings and in communicating.   Over ten years I have simplified Huthwaite's excellent categorization into nine behaviours and linked them to the personal styles (pages 28–30):

'ANALYSE' skills for CLARITY		EXAMPLE
1. **INFORMING**	provides facts and opinions.	'It's now 2.30'
2. **QUESTIONING**	seeks additional information or ideas from someone else.	'When should we leave?'
3. **CHECKING**	makes sure that the content or implication of what has just been said has been fully understood.	'So you think we should go right away?'
'BOND' skills for TEAMWORK		
4. **RESPONDING**	provides a positive or negative reaction to another's contribution.	'Great idea!'
5. **BUILDING**	develops a course of action suggested by someone else.	'...then we can join the others'
6. **BRINGING IN**	consciously invites someone else to take part in the discussion.	'What do you think, Fred?'
'COMMAND' skills for RESULTS		
7. **SUGGESTING**	proposes a particular course of action.	'Let's go'
8. **INTERRUPTING**	limits ability of others to contribute to the discussion.	'I feel we...' 'Not now, Jim'
9. **SUMMARIZING**	focuses on the key elements of what has been said by bringing them together in a concise form.	'So we are all agreed to go now.'

These nine behaviours enable you to identify precisely what is happening in any discussion, and to modify your behaviour accordingly. They also enable you to move effectively between the three styles by adjusting your verbal behaviour.   Each behaviour has advantages and disadvantages which help you to select according to the needs of each situation:

ADVANTAGES	DISADVANTAGES	
Enables discussion based on data rather than emotion.	Information can be excessive and may not be correct.	1.
Ensures that critical information is not overlooked.	Takes time and can encourage provision of too much data.	2.
Avoids misunderstanding and demonstrates interest in what has just been said.	Slows down momentum of discussion and can be seen as nitpicking.	3.
People know where they stand, and energy level rises.	Misunderstandings and personal or uncontrolled reactions can result.	4.
Encourages 'breakthrough' ideas and team solutions.	Can be an intellectual challenge and lose touch with reality.	5.
Increases range of contributions and commitment.	Can cause delay, distraction and embarrass some people.	6.
Encourages action and progress towards a result.	Can have too many ideas to handle and bring about competition between ideas.	7.
Curbs excessive and irrelevant contributions.	Stops worthwhile contributions and can cause frustration.	8.
Encourages focused discussion and likelihood of agreed action.	Difficult to recall past contributions briefly and accurately.	9.

5. The method of learning

The book is laid out with explanations of each skill on the left and blank forms on the right for you to complete step-by-step in parallel with each explanation. You will find it helpful to read through *the whole* of the explanation for each chapter on the left before starting to complete the practice forms on the right, in order to see each step in its context.

In the practice forms on the right you will always be asked for information from *your own work situation*, so that the effort you put in will be repaid by consistently providing you with practical material for later use *on the job*. At the bottom of each box on every practice sheet you will find sample answers to guide you towards your own answer.

The explanation and practice sheets for each of the three skills are followed first by a completed worksheet (page 54), questionnaire (page 72) or checklist (page 90), and then by an identical blank format for you to fill in for yourself.

The *worksheet* and *checklist* are designed to pull together all the steps of each process and to act as a summary of the skill you have just worked through; they are also useful reminders of the skill as you prepare to practise. The *questionnaire* acts as a checklist for each skill *after* practising, and should be completed as soon as possible after the experience.

After the open learning practice available in this workbook, first section-by-section, step-by-step, and then on each summary worksheet, *immediate practice* at work to secure the skills is most important. Remember that valuable opportunities for practice also exist *outside* the working environment in low risk domestic or social situations.

For example domestic and personal issues particularly benefit from the application of 'focusing on the key issues', because they have probably developed over a long period and are very emotionally charged.   Meetings of social – or sporting – groups are rarely run effectively, and how many groups are regularly kept informed of progress or plans?

You do not learn to drive a car or to play a musical instrument without *regular practice* – learning the skills of management has the same requirement.

The process works like this:

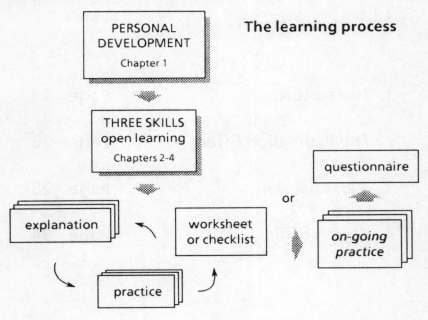

Before working through the three skills covered by this workbook, it is important to consider key elements of your personal development that will help to ensure that the skills learning is well-founded and effective.

Chapter One

PERSONAL DEVELOPMENT

PERSONAL DEVELOPMENT

1. The culture

The management climate and culture at work is critical to successful personal development. The role model we provide for our staff or the example of operational behaviour that our manager sets for us creates an environment that can make or break our willingness and our ability to develop ourselves.

A culture of development requires *everyone* to be kept informed. A management perspective is developed by a *regular* supply of information about the business, its objectives, its problems, its products, being available so that individuals can identify with the business and its future. Understanding business information requires education *over a period of time*; it takes time – and patience – for people not familiar with the business to develop understanding and a positive response.

A culture of *professional* learning is also required. Personal growth can only take place if the technical and professional needs of all staff are shared and efforts made to respond to those needs. This does not simply mean sending people away on external training courses. A great deal of professional and management development can be gained by means of capable internal *coaching* and advice.

Of course coaching and the need for professional development is not only beneficial to the individual concerned, but, by developing the competence base of the whole workforce, enables the unit to compete in a business environment that is constantly demanding state-of-the-art methods and technology.

But the individual's developmental needs depend on the personal information available to the manager, and on the conclusions he or she draws from it.   Performance information from meetings, appraisals etc is useless unless it is handled with integrity by the responsible manager.

The *systematic approach* in dealing with all management information is a discipline which creates a climate of trust and confidence. It is dependent on clear goals or a mission statement being thought through and communicated to all involved. This provides a unifying perspective against which all work can be carried out. It leads to integrated roles and targets, Volume 1, *Managing Operations*, and to the maintenance of agreed standards.

The benefits of the systematic approach in management is perhaps best understood when viewed as a situation in which it is *not* deployed. People do not know what they are supposed to be doing, tasks are allocated arbitrarily and performance is judged upon a whim. Response to information is spontaneous, often dependent on a passing mood. Decisions are made 'on the hoof' – 'that's what managers are for'! – and problems supposedly resolved by 'gut feel'.

Instead, we are looking to managers carefully considering the facts in any situation, checking the evidence, specifying criteria and weighing up pros and cons against standards.

But the systematic use of information does not mean pages of computer printouts, or an obsession with 'bottom-line' considerations. Information, like everything else in management, requires balance. Balance is largely determined by clear objectives or purposes. What is the purpose of the information, and is it continuing to fulfil that purpose at an affordable cost – in terms of time as well as money?

Information is the life-blood of management. Coming in, it provides perspective and control, going out it reassures and motivates. This twin dimension is readily available at a well-run *meeting*. Relationships are revealed and data can be cross-questioned, reactions can be evaluated and ideas developed.

Given effective leadership, a meeting can supply all the information for problem solving and decision making a manager needs (*MCI Units 8 and 9*); *without* those leadership skills, it can be the biggest waste of time and money ever invented by man! Without effective meetings, real teamwork is impossible.

The self-teach open learning method of this workbook will help you to develop your confidence in responding to your information needs and to those of your staff. It will allow you to develop your own skills as and when you need them, in your own time and at your own pace. Performance will then continuously improve in an environment in which information flows naturally in to you and out from you, creating an increasingly informed, committed and responsive workforce.

2.   The Pygmalion Effect

The way management is performed around us creates a culture in which we feel able – or not – to develop our full potential. Similarly the right *attitude* is critical to managing ourselves and other people, and the development of a *positive* attitude is essential before setting out to acquire new skills.

Positive thinking has been proved to be critical to success; positive expectations of an outcome increase the likelihood of a successful result. The conscious development of positive thinking and of high expectations of ourselves and others can have a remarkable effect on our confidence, our relationships and our success. Enthusiasm is an essential pre-requisite of effective communication.

And yet the most natural response to unknown people and uncertain situations is *negative*. So often, both individually and in groups, we display negative rather than positive responses. Often it is because we are uncertain.   Uncertainty – lack of information – leads to fear and fear to expectations of failure. We can soon find that it becomes a *self-fulfilling prophecy*.

To manage effectively therefore we have continuously to overcome uncertainty with a regular and reliable supply of essential *information*, and then to make *every effort to be objective* with the information we have received. Information, suggestions or advice, can so easily provide us with disparate messages, depending on our attitude, our expectations – and our opinion of the information *source*.

Are we capable of being *dispassionate* about information, drawing rational conclusions, despite the negative expectations that we or those around us may possess of the data being provided?

2. The Pygmalion Effect

2.1 *Write down a recent situation in which you received some significant management information:*

Finance wanted our budgets by end of June and a cut of 5%

2.2 *What was your attitude to-wards this information, and/or the source of the information?*	
	Typical of Finance to want it at start of holiday period; no way can we take a further 5% cut!
What was the effect of your attitude on the action you took as a result of receiving this information?	
	I didn't 'sell' it to my team, and so get their commitment to providing the figures
2.3 *If your approach was negative, how might you have been more positive towards the information or the person who supplied it?*	
	Boss had explained the reasons and I had accepted. I knew reason for delay and should have explained

3.   Personal style

Our ability to manage some situations and not others, to manage some people and not others, is partly a question of the sort of person we are, our personal style. If we understood more about our style it would help us to know and to develop our natural strengths and to accept or overcome our limitations.

The three styles we developed are very simple and represent the basis of 'what makes people tick'. They first emerged as a result of considering an interesting model of motivation, which exactly reflected the result of the research we were doing at the time into leadership styles and the means of identifying *potential* managers.

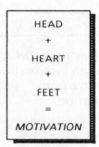

HEAD
+
HEART
+
FEET
=
MOTIVATION

The first distinct style is **'Analyse'** (or 'Head') to represent the thinking, analytical type of person; the second is **'Bond'** (or 'Heart'), the feeling, caring type of person; the third is **'Command'** (or 'Feet'), the active, results-orientated type of person.

Each style can be summed up as follows:

'ANALYSE' (or 'Head')
Values logic and distrusts subjective judgements; able to provide considered and rational arguments; keen to see rules and procedures applied.

'BOND' (or 'Heart')
Conscious of the importance of mutual understanding and stresses the benefits of working with people; seeks to get the best out of others by trust and encouragement.

'COMMAND' (or 'Feet')

Likes to be in control of people and events, quickly responding to job demands and opportunities; trusts own judgement and acts on conclusions; inclined to use incentives and sanctions to influence results.

A high-scoring 'Analyse' type of person is likely to be quiet and methodical, a conscientious administrator who likes to get things right. A predominantly 'Bond' person is likely to be open with emotions and conscious of the importance of other people, a visible carer with individuals or inside a team. A 'Command' person is likely to be impatient for results and to know instinctively what needs doing, an entrepreneur or 'born organizer'.

But people rarely fit a style description exactly. People are usually a mixture of the three styles, generally of just two of them. *Few of us have the capacity to spread equally across all three.* We often have one which is an area of weakness which tends to ruin our all round performance, but which provides a focus for our personal development.

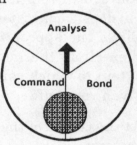

There are of course many current methods of identifying personal style. Generally, though, they provide you with an interesting profile but no plan of action to aid your development, and almost certainly no links to learnable management skills.

However, one of the benefits of the 'toolkit' approach is that the skills within the toolkit can be re-assembled into different shapes for different purposes. The skills in the Personal Development Toolkit overleaf have been re-assembled to match the most appropriate style.

'Analyse' covers the *information*-providing skills ('monitoring', 'clarifying', 'specifying' and 'focusing'), skills associated with individual thinking processes.

'Bond' covers skills associated with being with *people* ('making more of others' ideas', 'giving and receiving feedback', 'communicating' and 'meeting'), skills most effective when done with openness and feeling.

The 'Command' skills are all related to taking *action* and getting results ('persuading', 'planning action', 'making decisions' and 'developing performance').

In the style questionnaire overleaf you are asked to consider yourself in relation to 12 straightforward statements. How far does each statement represent a fair description of you? Circle the appropriate number against each statement, and then circle the number in the next column to indicate the extent to which you would like to change the rating you have given yourself.

At the centre of the personal development model opposite are the core skills of 'specifying targets and standards', 'making more of others' ideas' and 'planning action' (in italics). These are the essence of the integrated style – **'Drive'** – which contains elements of the other three styles. It is the basis of a balanced *leadership* – and of an effective management – style:

Clear and positive in thinking towards future possibilities; capable of generating enthusiasm and a flexible approach to achieving results; is sensitive to others' feelings and expectations and inspires teamwork.

'Drive' style requires the ability to move between 'Head', 'Heart' and 'Feet', to be able to adjust your personal style according to the changing needs of the situation.

Personal Development Toolkit

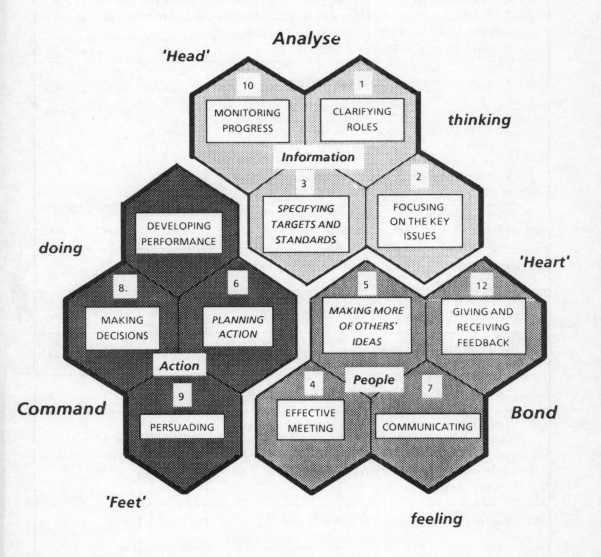

© PETER GRAINGER 1994

Style Questionnaire

3.1 Score the extent to which the following statements apply to you NOW on a scale 1–5 (1 = Not you; 3 = Yes, but...; 5 = Fully you). Circle the number (1 2 3 4 5) which is most appropriate to you. Then circle the number in the next column to indicate the extent to which you would like to change this rating:

	'NOW'	'CHANGE'
1. You think carefully about what needs doing and why.	1 2 3 **4** 5	+2 +1 **0** -1 -2
2. You can be relied upon to get things into perspective.	1 2 **3** 4 5	**+2** +1 0 -1 -2
3. You are concerned that things should be done correctly.	1 2 3 **4** 5	+2 +1 **0** -1 -2
4. You work effectively in groups.	1 2 3 4 5	+2 **+1** 0 -1 -2
5. You respond positively to other people's ideas.	1 2 **3** 4 5	+2 **+1** 0 -1 -2
6. You get people organized for action.	1 2 3 **4** 5	+2 **+1** 0 -1 -2
7. You consistently keep people informed.	1 **2** 3 4 5	**+2** +1 0 -1 -2
8. You have no difficulty making up your mind.	1 2 3 4 **5**	+2 +1 **0** -1 -2
9. You always seem to be able to get others to do what you want.	1 2 3 **4** 5	+2 **+1** 0 -1 -2
10. You make sure you know how things are progressing.	1 2 **3** 4 5	**+2** +1 0 -1 -2
11. You make the most of what is available.	1 2 3 **4** 5	+2 **+1** 0 -1 -2
12. You prefer to deal with people face-to-face.	1 2 **3** 4 5	+2 **+1** 0 -1 -2

Bold type represents the scores in the example on page 35.   © *PETER GRAINGER 1994*

3.2 *To consider your own relationship to the three basic styles transfer your 'Now' scores and the 'Change' scores from the questionnaire according to the number of each statement. Add up the total 'Now' scores and highlight the most significant 'Change' scores, keeping the two sets separate:*

		'NOW' SCORES		'CHANGE' SCORES

'Analyse'

1. You think carefully about what needs doing and why.	[ ]	3	[ ]	+1
3. You are concerned that things should be done correctly.	[ ]	2	[ ]	(+2)
10. You make sure you know how things are progressing.	[ ]	3	[ ]	(+2)
2. You can be relied upon to get things into perspective.	[ ]	4	[ ]	0
TOTAL	[ ]	12		

'Bond'

7. You consistently keep people informed.	[ ]	3	[ ]	+1
12. You prefer to deal with people face-to-face.	[ ]	5	[ ]	0
5. You respond positively to other people's ideas.	[ ]	4	[ ]	0
4. You work effectively in groups.	[ ]	4	[ ]	+1
TOTAL	[ ]	16		

'Command'

9. You always seem to be able to get others to do what you want.	[ ]	4	[ ]	+1
6. You get people organized for action.	[ ]	3	[ ]	(+2)
8. You have no difficulty making up your mind.	[ ]	3	[ ]	+1
11. You make the most of what is available.	[ ]	4	[ ]	+1
TOTAL	[ ]	14		

Example scores are in **bold type**; the resulting profile appears on Page 35.

4. Style profile

You should now have a total score for each style, but these totals do not tell you very much until you see them graphically in relation to each other. It is this inter-relationship that is important, not the size of the totals produced.

By transferring your total scores for 'Analyse', 'Bond' and 'Command' on to the model on page 37 your profile will normally emerge as a triangle with a 'pull' towards one particular area of skills. (The letters 'CA', 'AC' etc will help you to communicate the direction of that pull to others.)

In the example opposite the person's *strengths* lie bottom left towards 'Command'. The skills in that area are 'persuading', 'making decisions' and 'planning action'. The area on the *opposite* side to the shape of the profile (shaded) covers skills from AB round to BC. These are likely to be among the skills to concentrate on as personal development priorities. 'Focusing on the key issues' and 'communicating' are of course covered in this workbook.

If the triangle of your profile is equilateral you are probably 'Drive' style, or at least have the potential to be. But it is more likely that there will be a 'pull' in one particular direction, a 'skew' towards one style or perhaps two. This skew will be in the direction of your *natural* strengths, and the skills on the model *nearest* to that skew will identify a particular area of confidence and competence for you.

Example of Completed Style Profile

4.1 Transfer your total 'Now' scores for each 'style' from 3.2 on page 33:

'Analyse':   'Bond':   'Command':

| 14 | 12 | 17 |

Circle or cross the appropriate number on the model below, and join up the points to produce a style profile. Circle those skills with the highest 'Change' scores.

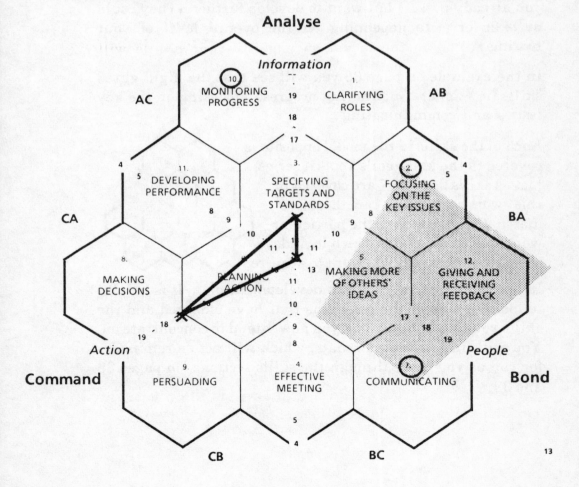

The skills on the model *furthest away* from the shape of your profile are those that you probably do not find easy to carry out; you may therefore need to concentrate on them particularly as part of your personal development.

To check out your priorities, highlight your highest 'Change' scores from Section 3.2 on page 33 by ringing or underlining the appropriate number on the model opposite. These may be skills which you find difficult and want to improve or skills you already possess but want to develop further. (They could be +2s or +1s depending on the overall level of your scoring.)

In the example on page 35 you will see that the highlighted skills (ie +2s) are 'monitoring progress', 'focusing on the key issues' and 'communicating'.

Each of the skills in the model opposite is covered in the Manager's Toolkit series, just as skills 2, 4 and 7 are covered in this workbook. You can therefore match your needs with the particular workbook in the series which includes the particular skills you want to acquire.

In order to focus on your own development plan, it is helpful to make a note of the strengths that have emerged and the skills you find difficult that you now intend to concentrate on. You will find suitable formats, which will act as reminders for you as you move through the skills sections, on pages 38 and 39.

Style Profile

4.2 Write your total 'Now' scores for each 'style' from 3.2 on page 33 in the boxes below:

'Analyse': **'Bond'**: **'Command'**:

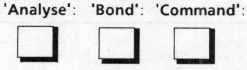

Circle or cross the appropriate number on the model below, and join up the points to produce a style profile. Then highlight the skills with the highest 'Change' scores:

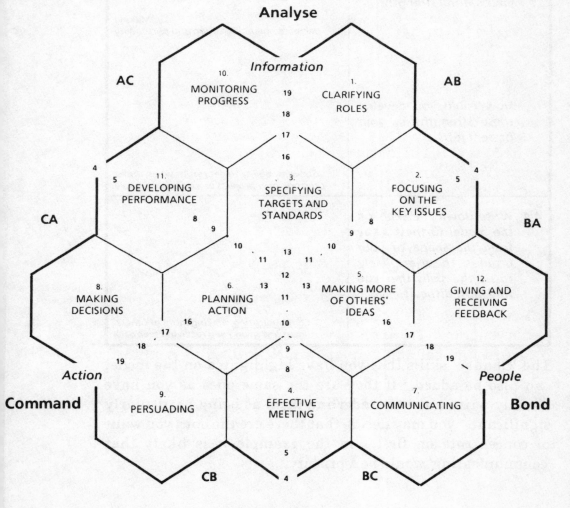

© PETER GRAINGER 1994

From consideration of your profile, identify your strongest skills in the space below and consider ways of developing them. Then make a note of the skills furthest away from the shape of your profile, and confirm that these are the skills you want to improve.

4.3 Write down the skills closest to the shape of your profile which you also scored highly. These are your natural strengths. How could you develop these strengths in your present job?	*Making decisions, planning action and persuading* *Show my ability to get results when under pressure, new projects or a negotiating role*
4.4 Write down the skills on the model furthest away from the shape of your profile. These are likely to be the skills that you find most difficult:	<u>*Communicating,*</u> *making more of others' ideas and giving and receiving feedback*

The 'Change' skills that you have highlighted on the model can also be added. If they are the same ones as you have already written down, underline them as being particularly significant – you may decide that these are the ones you want to concentrate on first. In the example it is likely that 'communicating' would be a priority.

4.4 (continued) Add the high-lighted 'Change' skills, underlining any on page 38 that are the same: *How committed are you to improving these skills?*	*Monitoring and focusing* *In last appraisal boss told me to take time to think and to keep my people with me*

5. Personal development plan

In the examples in Sections 4.4 'communicating' and 'focusing on the key issues' are covered by this workbook, and so these two skills can be developed with the help of the skills pages which follow. 'Monitoring progress' is covered in Volume 4, *Managing Resources*.

The person with the profile on page 35 may therefore decide, in addition to the skills in this workbook, to develop the other skills in Volume 4, 'making decisions' and 'persuading' in addition to 'monitoring progress', which has already been highlighted as a 'Change' skill.

The model of the skills in each volume of the Manager's Toolkit series on Page 13 is reproduced on page 40 as an on-going reference for you at the start of the skills pages.

You will observe, as you move through the skills pages, that at the end of each chapter a model shows the skills in the Manager's Toolkit which most closely relate to the particular skills in this book.

On page 58 you will see that 'making decisions' and 'monitoring progress' from Volume 4, *Managing Resources* (see below) link to 'focusing'. On page 76 'monitoring progress' links to 'effective meeting', and on page 93 'persuading' and 'making decisions' relate to 'communicating'. There is a natural skills progression from 'managing information' to 'managing resources', and so that workbook could be a logical next step.

But a more beneficial *personal development* plan could emerge from the importance of *'making more of others' ideas'* which links to *all* of the skills in this book. The profile on page 35 suggests there is a need to develop the 'People' skills of 'ideas' and 'feedback', and so Volume 2, *Managing People*, is likely to be a more challenging option.

The 'Information' skills of 'focusing on the key issues', 'effective meeting' and 'communicating' now follow, with explanations on the left and practice activities on the right.

Chapter Two

FOCUSING ON
THE KEY ISSUES

FOCUSING ON THE KEY ISSUES

Focusing on the key issues enables you to break a large, confused and unmanageable task or problem into smaller units, so that you can get it into perspective and take appropriate action.

1. Identifying the factors

Taking appropriate management action depends on having the right information to hand (*MCI Unit 8.0*). But frequently the information we have is in a confused, disorganised and random shape, and in no condition to help us to make a considered decision. 'Focusing' is a multi-purpose process which breaks up unclear issues into smaller units for action.

It can be used equally effectively in groups or individually, lending itself particularly well to visual display in a group problem-solving situation.

The first step with any problem is to *write it down* as precisely as you can, and then be prepared to re-write your initial statement until it represents what is *actually going wrong*. (Problem analysis is dealt with more fully in 'Monitoring Progress' in Volume 4, *Managing Resources*.) The process can also apply to a *task* which is initially so unclear that you cannot see where to begin in taking action.

To break the problem or task into manageable units of action, you next list down all the *factors* you can think of that are currently *helping* and *hindering* the situation you have

1. Identifying the factors

Do you have a problem, task or activity which seems to be too large and confused for you to be able to take appropriate action?

1.1   Write down the problem or task as you now see it:

> *Staff are unhappy about the new organization*

1.2   Keep re-writing what you have just written until it seems to represent either what is actually going wrong or precisely what you have to achieve.

> *Bill's staff not accepting being moved into my section after he took early retirement*

described. These are factors which are contributing to the problem, possible causes of the unsatisfactory situation, *and* factors which are preventing it getting worse, redeeming features, allies actually helping you to make progress.

The process enables you to create a *balanced* picture, the 'equilibrium' of the situation at this particular point in time. It is surprising how much more *positive* the situation appears, and how many more *courses of action* become apparent, as a result of using the process. It represents a very practical application of the positive 'Pygmalion Effect' (see pages 26–7).

Remember that, although you are creating a balanced picture between the 'helps' and the 'hinders', the factors do not counter-balance each other across the page.

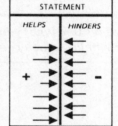

Write a summary of your problem or task statement, at the top of a page or flipchart, and then draw a line down the middle of the remainder of the page, heading the left-hand column, *'Helps'*, and the right-hand column, *'Hinders'*. You then list as many factors as you can think of that are relevant to the issue under each heading. They are likely to occur to you randomly on either side of the line, and to be nouns or phrases at this stage; courses of action (ie verbs) come later.

If you are having difficulty thinking of factors, ask yourself *who* or *what* are helping or hindering the situation. *When*, *where* and *how much* (see 'Specifying Targets and Standards' in Volume 1, *Managing Operations*) become, for instance, timescales or time of year factors, location or facility factors, and factors relating to cost or quantity. Some of these 'extra' thoughts can turn out to be surprisingly significant – they are also likely to be new dimensions to the problem.

1.3	Write the amended statement of your problem or task at the top of a blank piece of paper with a line underneath it:	Bill's staff not accepting transfer to my section	

Bill's staff not accepting transfer to my section

HELPS	HINDERS
- Sections are compatible	- Staff liked Bill
- Cost saving	- Bill 'Mr. Nice Guy'
- My boss very keen	- No warning of change
- Boss won't mess about	- Pressure on Bill to go
- Challenge for me to fix	- Seen as 'take over'
- No problems with them in past	- Staff numbers falling
- Boss supports me	- I'm 'new broom'
- I understand their work	- Bill's long service
- Opportunity for me to show I can manage	- I'm 'blue eyed-boy'
- Boss wants cost savings	- Staff's future insecure
- Staff normally sensible	- No explanation given
- Bill known to be too easy-going with his staff	- Other managers going
- My staff working well	- Bill reluctant at first
- Happening elsewhere	- Past friction between our sections
- Boss keen to develop new managers	- They don't know me
- Helpful individually	- Bill very technically competent
	- Negative thinking all round

1.3 Write the amended statement of your problem or task at the top of a blank piece of paper with a line underneath it:

1.4 Draw a vertical line down the centre of the page, and write 'helps' above the left-hand column and 'hinders' above the right-hand column:

1.5 List under the appropriate headings all the factors you can think of that are currently helping and hindering the situation you have written at the top of the page:

1.6 To get you started, you may like to write the first help and hinder factors that occur to you in the columns below:

HELPS	*HINDERS*

2. Giving them shape

It is likely that you will have produced more factors than you can see your way to actioning. The brain can usually separate out about five or six discrete items. If you have more than that number each side of the centre line you will probably need to sort and group them with other similar factors .

Some people can very quickly sort items of information into appropriate headings – 'top down' – like producing file headings for a pile of random papers. Most people, however, prefer to sort the information more systematically – 'bottom up' – by matching up related topics, and then giving those groups of topics suitable headings.

For example, the list on page 45 includes the following 'hinder' factors:

> *'Seen as take-over'*
> *'Staff numbers falling'*
> *'Staff future insecure'*
> *'Past friction between sections,'*

and a suitable heading for them might be *'Bill's staff feeling insecure'*. Notice that the heading is negative because we are grouping *hinder* factors together.

Identify the first help factor as 'A', look for another factor which seems to be related and mark that 'A' as well. Then go on until you have exhausted the potential of that particular grouping. It is worth making a note as you go along of what you have in mind as the meaning of each heading. Jot it down somewhere informally so that you can come back to it at the end to produce a more precise definition of each particular group. You then proceed to factors under 'B' etc until all helps and then hinders have been accounted for.

2. Giving them shape

Can you determine which of the factors you should take action on first?

2.1 *If there are too many factors to prioritise, try to group them under suitable headings.*	
Write here the first headings that occur to you as you look through your list of factors:	ORGANIZATION, CHANCE FOR ME, BOSS, STAFF'S VIEW, THE BUSINESS

2.2 *Try to improve the headings you have just written down, making sure that the helps are positive and the hinders are negative:*

A ....   F ....

   ....

B ....   G ....

   ....

C ....   H ....

   ....

D ....   I ....

   ....

E ....   J ....

For examples of headings see Section 2.3.

The meaning of each heading is extremely important because they become the *actions* you are going to take, so the more precise they are the more effective and relevant will be the action plan you produce.

Make sure that the headings of *hinder* factors are all negative, and the headings for the *helps* are positive. This will help you later to add appropriate *maximizing* or *minimizing* verbs to each to turn the factors into action.

When you are happy with all the headings, they can be transferred onto the Focusing Worksheet on pages 56–7 which is laid out in the form of a 'fishbone' (see the example on pages 54–5). The 'fishbone' is based on the well-known 'Ishikawa' diagram, but turned into a vertical plane for ease of use on flipcharts and normal A4 configuration.

The fishbone shape enables you to see the issue in the perspective of 6–8 sections. If time permits, it is usually worthwhile to put the individual help and hinder factors under their respective headings to check that they are appropriate, and that they link to each other in representing a true picture of the overall problem or task.

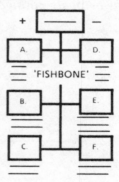

We have just been through a critical process in the management of information. We have created shape and perspective out of randomly collected data, a process which is required again and again in the day-to-day life of a manager. In preparing a report or a presentation, in clarifying a role or summarizing a meeting, we are doing the same thing with our information – creating a structure and a shape in order to provide meaning and appropriate action.

2.3 If appropriate headings do not occur to you easily, try linking similar factors together by adding reference letters, and gradually develop headings for each group as they come together.

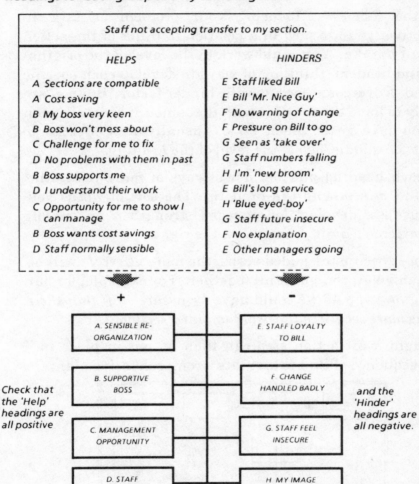

Staff not accepting transfer to my section.

HELPS	HINDERS
A Sections are compatible	E Staff liked Bill
A Cost saving	E Bill 'Mr. Nice Guy'
B My boss very keen	F No warning of change
B Boss won't mess about	F Pressure on Bill to go
C Challenge for me to fix	G Seen as 'take over'
D No problems with them in past	G Staff numbers falling
B Boss supports me	H I'm 'new broom'
D I understand their work	E Bill's long service
C Opportunity for me to show I can manage	H 'Blue eyed-boy'
B Boss wants cost savings	G Staff future insecure
D Staff normally sensible	F No explanation
	E Other managers going

+   **-**

Check that the 'Help' headings are all positive

A. SENSIBLE RE-ORGANIZATION	E. STAFF LOYALTY TO BILL
B. SUPPORTIVE BOSS	F. CHANGE HANDLED BADLY
C. MANAGEMENT OPPORTUNITY	G. STAFF FEEL INSECURE
D. STAFF POTENTIAL	H. MY IMAGE WRONG

and the 'Hinder' headings are all negative.

2.4 Write the headings in the boxes on the Focusing Worksheet which follows on pages 56–7, adding the appropriate factors under each. You now have a 'fishbone' which will enable you get your problem or task into perspective so that you can see what action to take.

3.   Planning the action

With the factors influencing your problem or task in perspective, you are now in a position to think of the action you want to take. You could work at the level of the original helps and hinders, thinking of ways to develop each specific help and to overcome each specific hinder factor. But you are unlikely to have time to deal with that amount of detail, even after you have sorted them. So it is usually most effective to work at the middle 'level', the level of the *headings*.

Take each heading and list down ways of *maximizing* the helps and *minimizing* the hinders. The sort of words you might use are 'develop', 'encourage', 'strengthen' on the left and 'overcome', 'limit', 'remove' on the right.

The more specific the added verbs, the more effective will be your plan when you put it all together. For example, for our heading on page 46 we could have *'re-assure staff that their future is more secure in the new combined section'.*

Each significant action step can then be put in place in a logical sequence of events to create a comprehensive plan:

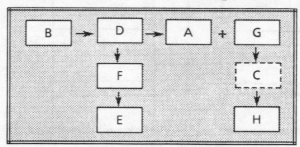

Sometimes actions link together to form a single more significant step in your overall plan (as A and G on page 53), or an action can be omitted from the final shape of your plan as a low priority step that is never likely to get actioned.

3. Planning the action

Can you now see what action to take in solving your problem or achieving the task?

3.1   *List suitable maximizing phrases for each 'help' heading and minimizing phrases for each 'hinder' heading to create the basis of a plan of action:*

HELPS   HINDERS

A .... □   *F* .... □

B .... □   *G* .... □

C .... □   *H* .... □

D .... □   *I* .... □

E .... □   *J* .... □

A. EXPLOIT SENSE OF THE RE-ORGANIZATION,

ie explain to the staff the justification for the organization

E. MAKE MOST OF STAFF'S LOYALTY TO BILL,

ie acknowledge and build on Bill's achievements; their loyalty will transfer to me in time

It is important that you make sure that each action step in your plan is eventually written as a precise 'end result' target or objective.

If you suspect that you will not have enough time to carry out all the actions that emerge from the 'Focusing' process, you will probably need to *prioritize* the steps to make sure you spend your time on the most important.

Managing Operations, Volume 1 in the Manager's Toolkit series, provides you with a practical planning worksheet and a simple method of prioritizing. The skill required to turn actions into targets and standards, so that you and those involved in your plan know precisely what you have to achieve, is also contained in that workbook.

Any of the action steps that have emerged through focusing may need further breaking down. If one of them is still a large area of action, you could create another fishbone at the lower level.

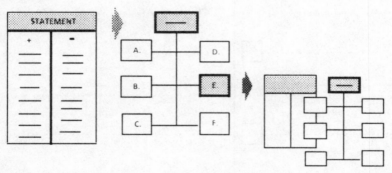

Or if there is an area of the problem or task in which you do not know how to proceed, you might consider involving other people in generating ideas, or even a short session of 'brainstorming'. (Volume 2, *Managing People*, contains the requisite skills in the chapter, 'Making More of Others' Ideas.)

3.2   Put the actions into a logical sequence by adding numbers to the boxes in Section 3.1, and then try to lay out the steps to create an integrated action plan:

EXAMPLE:

MANAGEMENT

C. Take trouble to prepare a plan and get it right.   →   B. Discuss plan with boss and ensure support.

NEW STAFF

A. Explain justification for re-organization

E. Acknowledge & build on Bill's achievements; loyalty will transfer to me in time.   ←   G. and re-assure staff of more security in combined section.   ←   F. Respect staff's feelings and take time to explain.

H. Talk about my role and our mission at joint meeting with my staff.   ALL STAFF   →   D. Talk to each about work with positive expectations.

FOCUSING WORKSHEET

Write a statement of the problem or task to be dealt with, and list the relevant help and hinder factors. Group them into a 'fishbone' structure ready for appropriate

STATEMENT
Staff are not accepting being moved into my section after Bill was put under pressure to take early retirement.

HELPS

A.   RE-ORGANIZATION MAKES BUSINESS SENSE   `4`

- Sections are compatible
- Cost saving
- Bill was too easy-going with staff
- It is happening elsewhere - not unique to Bill's section

B.   MY BOSS IS VERY SUPPORTIVE   `2`

- Boss insists on the change
- Doesn't mess about once decided
- Supports me
- Wants the cost savings

C.   MANAGEMENT OPPORTUNITY FOR ME   `1`

- Willing to develop new managers

- A challenge for me to fix
- Can demonstrate that I can 'manage'
- My current staff are working well

D.   STAFF HAVE POTENTIAL TO COOPERATE   `8`

- No problems with them in past
- I understand their work
- They are sensible people
- Helpful individually

maximizing or minimizing action, with helps on the left and hinders on the right. Decide on the sequence of steps or priority actions, and number the boxes accordingly.

HINDERS

E. *STAFF'S LOYALTY TO BILL*

| 6 |

- *Staff liked Bill*
- *'Mr Nice Guy'*
- *Long service with company*
- *Bill reluctant to leave at first*
- *Very technically competent*

F. *CHANGE WAS HANDLED BADLY*

| 3 |

- *No warning to staff*
- *Bill under pressure to go*
- *No explanation given*
- *Other managers going and upset*

G. *STAFF'S FEELING OF INSECURITY*

| 5 |

- *Seen as 'take over'*
- *Numbers already falling*
- *See own future as insecure*
- *Past friction between sections*

H. *I HAVE WRONG IMAGE WITH THEM*

| 7 |

- *I'm seen as 'new broom'*
- *Seen as boss's 'blue-eyed boy'*
- *They really don't know me*
- *Negative Pygmalion*

FOCUSING WORKSHEET

Write a statement of the problem or task to be dealt with, and list the relevant help and hinder factors. Group them into a 'fishbone' structure ready for appropriate

STATEMENT

HELPS

A.

B.

C.

D.

maximizing or minimizing action, with helps on the left and hinders on the right.
Decide on the sequence of steps or priority actions, and number the boxes accordingly.

HINDERS

E.

F.

G.

H.

Focusing on the Key Issues
links to other skills in
the Manager's Toolkit series

Each skill in this workbook not only links directly with other 'information' skills in the workbook (4), but also with other skills from the toolkit on page 13 (3, 5, 6, 8 and 10).

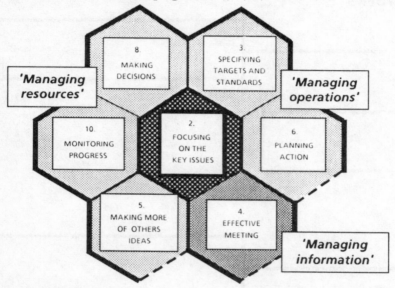

By means of monitoring (10) we identify that there is a problem to be resolved and that it needs to be broken into smaller units. Other people's ideas (5) may be required to identify factors and to build maximizing and minimizing actions.

The resulting draft plans are then turned into specific targets with standards (3), and finally built into an integrated and visible action plan (6), which may involve the use of *potential* help and hinder factors.

Decision making (8) requires 'focussed' alternatives for consideration, as well as weighing up the advantages and disadvantages of the final two or three 'best buys'.

Chapter Three

EFFECTIVE MEETING

EFFECTIVE MEETING

Effective meeting enables you to make the best use of bringing a group of people together for discussion.

1. Being prepared

Meetings are critical to the process of giving and receiving information, and yet we are all only too aware of the ineffectiveness of so many meetings. Meetings, like committees outside work, have become discredited because so often they are not run effectively, and inadequate results are seen to flow from them.

Even if we do not have direct responsibility for chairing a meeting, we do all have a responsibility for the effectiveness of the meetings we attend, and so can contribute to making them more effective. (*MCI Element 9.2*) A major contribution can be made before the meeting even gets under way.

The first key step for everyone involved is to be clear on the *purpose* of the particular meeting. *Why* are these particular people coming together at this particular time? The answer is usually to agree some courses of action, sometimes just to share some information. When the purpose is clear an agenda can be created.

It can be helpful, if you are to chair the meeting to jot down all the possible agenda items, and then identify which ones are essential to be dealt with at this particular meeting. You should make a note against each of roughly how long each item is likely to take, difficult though it is to get it right!

1. Being prepared

How carefully do you prepare for each meeting for which you are responsible?

			①	②	③
1.1	*Write down the purpose or purposes of your next meeting:* *What are you trying to achieve by bringing people to-gether on this occasion?*				
		Keep section informed how we are doing and get ideas on costs			
1.2	*Have you an agenda for this meeting? If you have, turn to 1.3.* *If not, write down your ideas for an agenda:* *Then in each column,* *① identify the relative importance of each item (with 1, 2, 3 etc):* *② add approximate timings for each item:* *③ add a number to denote an appropriate sequence for the priority items:*				

You can now assemble the items in an appropriate sequence, leaving the optional items to the end. If you can arrange it, the agenda – *your visible plan* – should be circulated to those attending a few days before the meeting. Everyone should be expected to give the agenda some preparatory thought before they attend – provided of course you have made sure that there is no ambiguity in the wording of each agenda item.

So often people attend meetings simply because they have always done so. How important is it that *everyone* attends every meeting and indeed every part of it? Who is *essential* to the items to be discussed? If the essential person cannot attend, there may be no point in having the meeting at that particular time; or perhaps the person concerned could just come for their particular item?

How are the people attending likely to behave? Who are likely to be your allies? Are there items which some people are likely to find contentious? Since meetings are made up of people interacting, it is important to give thought in advance to the way *they* are likely to behave and how *you* are going to react to that anticipated behaviour. It could even be important where you sit.

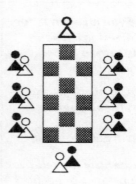

Time and location can have a significant effect on the success of a meeting. Is the room going to be large enough, warm enough, sufficiently well-lit late in the day etc? Do you need to get information copied to be handed out at or in advance of the meeting? Do you need to have visual aids, such as flipcharts or marker-boards, available to help clarify points. Will any refreshment be needed, and if so who is going to provide it? Such factors contribute to the motivation and efficiency of the group, and yet are so often overlooked or thought about too late.

1.3 When you have an agenda, write down the priority items in precise terms and in an appropriate sequence, adding the approximate time needed for each: Should you issue this agenda in advance of the meeting?

YES	NO

PRIORITY AGENDA ITEMS:	TIME REQD:
1.	
2.	
3.	
4.	
5.	
Identifying new methods of cost reduction in department	*½hr*

1.4 Who are the key people for these items, and how are they likely to behave? Is there any particular action you should be prepared to take as a result?

Jim for performance & cost info - check he can be there

1.5 If it is not a regular meeting, identify the most convenient date, time and location:

List any resources that need to be organized, eg information to be copied, equipment, refreshments, and who is going to provide them:

LOCATION:	DATE/TIME:

RESOURCES REQUIRED:	TO BE PROVIDED BY:
Copies of performance and annual costs info for all	*Jim*

2. Reaching consensus

A meeting is either about sharing information or reaching agreement on a particular course of action, (*MCI's 'to solve problems or make decisions'*).   A useful first step is to consider which items on the agenda *require* the group to reach agreement or consensus *now*. When will it be critical that the group as a whole sees eye-to-eye, and how are you going to make sure that it actually does?

People will more easily reach agreement if they understand the *background* and significance of the particular item to be discussed, especially items which are likely to be controversial. The context of the particular item should be put over briefly, clearly and in language appropriate to those present – enthusiasm for a successful outcome also helps!

People are more likely to understand and be committed to the progress of the discussion if they have first been consulted on the objective of that discussion. It is therefore as well to ensure that you have agreement on the purpose of the discussion before the discussion begins.

Clarity of information is essential to reaching consensus, to avoid people either thinking they disagree when they actually don't, or disagreeing on *unimportant* matters which they think are important. To aid clarification you may need to ask them questions or encourage others to ask questions.

Disagreement at a meeting is usually more productive than misunderstanding. Everyone knows where the person stands and can therefore do something about it. Disagreement is acceptable provided the person's motives are about achieving the group's objectives, and not personal.

People are normally willing to accept a decision that goes

2. Reaching consensus

With the knowledge you now have of the agenda, how important is it that you reach consensus at this meeting?

2.1 *Reaching consensus is particularly critical to which items on the agenda?*	*Current performance status and need to reduce costs*
2.2 *What results do you want from the discussion of these agenda items?* *How far are you prepared to let them come up with alternatives to your objectives?*	*Understanding of performance situation and commitment to improve - their ideas on methods, not results*
2.3 *How far will everyone understand the perspective and agree the objective of each of these items?* *What are the key messages you need to get across, and how are you going to do it?*	*Don't all accept need to reduce costs - charts of monthly rises and comparisons from Jim should demonstrate importance*

an effort has been made to understand what they have been saying. Everyone can contribute to this clarification process by regularly using the key skill of *checking* (see pages 18-19).

To make sure that everyone has their say, the person in the chair will usually have to *control* the proceedings. The most talkative may have to be restrained by sympathetic interruptions – acceptable if seen as aiding the purpose of the discussion and the need for *everyone* to be involved. A checking intervention, such as 'so what you are saying, Jim, is...' can effectively stop the flow – and show that you have been listening!

> **CHECKING**
> asks a question about what has just been said to ensure understanding of its content or implication.

Similarly the quietest person present may need to be brought into the discussion by a suitable question, eg 'What do you think, Mary?'. It is remarkable how often these people's contributions are particularly helpful because they have actually been listening to what has been said, and so frequently come up with a highly significant point.

It is important that someone questions and checks the common ground between them all, the specific areas of *agreement*, that emerge. It is all too easy for a group to highlight where they disagree and overlook the areas of agreement that actually exist between them. Intermittent *summaries* to highlight the agreement that has been reached step-by-step will also help to ensure progress.

Sometimes, when reaching consensus proves difficult to achieve, it is tempting to reach a conclusion by taking a vote. But it is often only a temporary and short-term solution because those who 'lose' the vote are unlikely to be satisfied with the outcome, and may look to reversing the decision at some future occasion.

2.4   *Of the nine interpersonal skills which you can use at a meeting (see 'Interpersonal Skills Checklist' on pages 18–19), which ones are you going to use to make sure that everyone has been listening, and has had an opportunity to speak?*

'Analyse':		*'Bond'*:		*'Command'*:	
INFORMING	☐	RESPONDING	☐	SUGGESTING	☐
QUESTIONING	☐	BUILDING	☐	INTERRUPTING	☐
CHECKING	☐	BRINGING IN	☐	SUMMARIZING	☐

2.5   *Who are the people that you are most likely to have to restrain by interrupting?*

David and Brian always have plenty to say!

Who are the people you are most likely to need to involve by bringing into the discussion?

Jane is often quiet in team meetings but has good ideas

2.6   *How are you going to guide them towards areas of agreement, rather than disagreement?*

Listen carefully, check understanding of each member's performance and record key points agreed

3.   Ensuring results

In the final analysis the chairman is responsible for getting results from the meeting. To do this he or she frequently has to take more conscious control than perhaps he or she would like. This may mean changing personal style, adjusting behaviour to the particular needs of each situation that arises in the course of the meeting.

If, for example, the meeting has to consider a complex new policy or procedure, 'Analyse' would be an appropriate style for the chairman to adopt (see page 28). In that situation the chairman would be likely to use behaviour which would provide or clarify the information required, ie 'informing', 'questioning' and 'checking' would be the appropriate behaviour.

If it is particularly important that the team works together on a particular item, 'Bond' would be the appropriate style, responding (and encouraging others to agree or disagree), building on others' ideas' and bringing in every member of the group. For more  details of these skills, see 'Making More of Others' Ideas' in Volume 2, *Managing People*).

If time is pressing and little progress is being made, 'Command' style behaviour needs to be adopted, ie suggesting how the group should proceed, interrupting to keep contributions brief, and summarizing the action steps that have been agreed.

Pressure of time can often prove useful in achieving agreement, and on occasions the chairman may be required to make a decision in the interests of reaching a conclusion in the time available. But remember that, unless the reason for the time pressure is made clear, the group may well not

3. Ensuring results

How are you going to make sure that you get results from this meeting?

3.1	Look back at the key agenda items in Section 1.3 which may require you to change your personal style to get results. Identify the items, and then the style and interpersonal skills (Section 2.4) that are likely to be most appropriate to each of them.

AGENDA ITEM	APPROPRIATE STYLE	APPROPRIATE INTERPERSONAL SKILLS
Review of Dept spend	*Analyse*	*Questioning and checking*

3.2	Identify any item(s) which would actually benefit from being constrained by time, considering whether you should change its place on the agenda: Make a note of any decisions which you may have to make in the interests of reaching a conclusion when time is short:	
		Cost reduction is so important. I'll have to make my own proposals if discussion takes too long or there is too much hassle at the end

accept such a unilateral decision. You might even consider putting the most controversial item *last* on the agenda – just before you break for lunch, for example!

It is very important that the members of a meeting are very clear what they have agreed. Action agreed needs to be summarized periodically during the meeting and *recorded* in some form. Individuals may be encouraged to make notes, formal minutes may be taken or a flipchart/marker-board used to display the agreement that has been reached.

> **SUMMARIZING**
>
> *focuses on the key elements of what has been said by bringing them together in a concise form, eg 'So we are agreed that we need to meet once more.'*

The method you choose will depend on the formality of the meeting, the availability of a suitable minute-taker and of a flip- or marker-board. Whatever method of recording is used, the results of the meeting should be apparent to all involved, and every action to be carried out by an individual noted by the individual concerned.

For the chairman to be able to *monitor* the results of the meeting, he or she needs either to make a brief note of the actions agreed, or have a more normal method in place. If progress against agreed action is reviewed each time a group meets, the discipline of meetings actually achieving results will become established – and the benefits of individual note-taking soon become apparent!

A meeting of course is also a very effective way of monitoring a team's progress against its tasks, each person's work in relation to the work of the others. Sharing performance information in this way helps to build cooperation within the team, as everyone appreciates the problems and achievements of those working around them.

3.3	How are you going to make sure that everyone is clear about what you agree during the meeting?	*Make time to summarize after each item & check individual note-taking*
	How will you record the key actions? Consider these methods and others:	NOTES BY MEMBERS ☐ ✓ MINUTES ☐ ✓ CHAIRMAN'S NOTES ☐ ✓ FLIPCHART ☐ ✓ MARKER-BOARD ☐ OTHER:
3.4	Identify the actions agreed at the last meeting on which you need to report and/or check progress:	*Check that all holiday schedules will be with me by end of week and identify any potential problem areas*
3.5	How far do you use meetings as a means of monitoring the team's performance? Is there anything further you could do?	*On agenda when there's a problem affecting everyone* *Make it regular first item on team meeting agendas*

MEETING WORKSHEET

Think back to the last meeting you chaired, and consider the effectiveness of your behaviour (the bracketed numbers refer to the sections in the 'Effective Meeting' unit):

Interpersonal Skills:

How effective do think you were in using these interpersonal skills?

Score: 'H' (too much use)
     'M' (about right)
     'L' (too little use)

TITLE AND DATE OF MEETING: *Monthly Team Meeting, 10 June*

INFORMING	H	RESPONDING	M	SUGGESTING	M
QUESTIONING	H	BUILDING	L	INTERRUPTING	M
CHECKING	M	BRINGING IN	L	SUMMARIZING	L

Effective Meeting:

1.	Was the time, place and opening appropriate to establishing a relaxed and positive atmosphere? (1.5)	*It was our usual time and place, but perhaps the morning would have meant they were fresher for such a difficult agenda.* *I didn't really give any perspective to the meeting as a whole. I moved from item to item as quickly as possible to have enough time for the discussion on cost reduction. I should have explained why it was important to move on.*
2.	Identify occasions when you adjusted your personal style to suit the particular needs of the situation: (3.1)	*When David started complaining about the difficulty of working in the present office layout.*
	What changes did you actually make?	*I switched to 'Command' – it was a distraction from the purpose of the meeting.*
	Which of the interpersonal skills did you use more or less? (2.4)	*I interrupted and reminded him of the agenda. I summarized the key points we had just agreed and suggested we move on.*

3.	How far did you make sure that everyone was actually listening? (2.4)	*There was a lot of questioning of Jim's information and of his answers. I checked their eventual understanding and acceptance of the figures. I need to encourage them to use checking behaviour in future similar situations.* *There was more note-taking than usual, so they must have been listening to something!*
4.	How far did you make sure that everyone had a chance to express their views? (2.5)	*Everyone had their say, I think, although Jim was unusually quiet later on – perhaps I should have brought him in to try to 'clear the air'.* *I should have interrupted Brian when he got on his hobby-horse, and forgot about bringing in Jane as I'd planned. She did eventually get involved by writing on the flipchart.*
5.	How effective were you at guiding members of the group towards agreement? (2.6)	*I didn't deliberately identify the common key points as I'd planned. They could have seriously disagreed over their relative cost performance, and above all I wanted consensus on methods of cost reduction.* *The flip-chart helped to focus our attention on areas of agreement.*
6.	How far were you able to summarize the key conclusions reached during the meeting? How did you make sure that those attending were later able to recall what had been agreed? (3.3)	*I reckon I was better at it this time - especially for the major items. I still need to do much more, but it takes so much effort of concentration and it's so easy to get involved oneself!* *The flipchart was critical, and Jane's checking that what she wrote was right helped a lot. Her notes based on what was written were sent to everyone, and will be the basis of the start of the next meeting.*

MEETING QUESTIONNAIRE

Think back to the last meeting you chaired, and consider the effectiveness of your behaviour (the bracketed numbers refer to the sections in the 'Effective Meeting' unit):

Interpersonal Skills:

How effective do think you were in using these inter-personal skills?

Score: 'H' (too much use)
       'M' (about right)
       'L' (too little use)

TITLE AND DATE OF MEETING:

INFORMING		RESPONDING		SUGGESTING	
QUESTIONING		BUILDING		INTERRUPTING	
CHECKING		BRINGING IN		SUMMARIZING	

Effective Meeting:

1. Was the time, place and opening appropriate to establishing a relaxed and positive atmosphere? (1.5)	
2. Identify occasions when you adjusted your personal style to suit the particular needs of the situation. (3.1) What changes did you actually make? Which of the interpersonal skills did you use more or less? (2.4)	

3.	How far did you make sure that everyone was actually listening? (2.4)	
4.	How far did you make sure that everyone had a chance to express their views? (2.5)	
5.	How effective were you at guiding members of the group towards agreement? (2.6)	
6.	How far were you able to summarize the key conclusions reached during the meeting? How did you make sure that those attending were later able to recall what had been agreed? (3.3)	

Effective Meeting
links to other skills in
the Manager's Toolkit series

Each skill in this workbook not only links directly with other 'information' skills in the workbook (2 and 7), but also with other skills from the toolkit on page 13 (3, 5, 6, and 10).

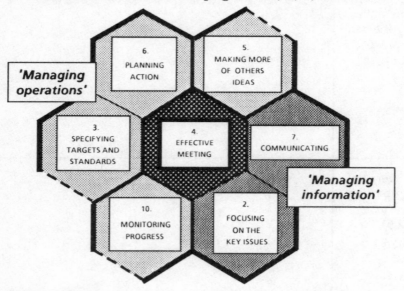

Others' ideas (5) are, of course, normally needed at meetings, and meetings are an essential method of monitoring individual and group performance (10). Targets, standards (3) and plans (6) affecting those attending the meeting are frequently the subject of much of the discussion at meetings.

Focusing (2) is an ideal process for clarifying situations in groups, and particularly in group problem-solving. Communicating (7) is frequently required at a meeting to provide perspective to what is being discussed, and the skills involved, as we have seen, are a natural development of the skills of effective meeting.

Chapter Four

COMMUNICATING

COMMUNICATING

Communicating helps you to make sure that everyone involved in an enterprise is regularly kept informed of progress, and so can understand and judge the real priorities for themselves.

1. Preparing the message

When helping participants on training programmes to resolve the problems they brought to the course, we found that poor communications was invariably one of the prime causes of their problem. Providing members of a team with the business context of their work has not generally been seen as an essential part of a manager's role in Britain, and yet it is a skill critical to the success of an enterprise.

Like appraisals, communicating is performed regularly and quite naturally by effective managers, but avoided at all costs by other managers who simply see such processes as a waste of a busy manager's time. One of the reasons for this apparent reluctance is that the skill is rather more difficult than it at first appears, and the word *communicating* has so many different meanings.

It is very important to appreciate the *purpose* of deploying this skill. Apart from motivation, people who are informed about the business context, the issues facing the organization, its priorities and key challenges, are much better able to determine their own priorities, to make less inappropriate decisions, and refer queries to their bosses less frequently. They work more cooperatively with their colleagues, aware of their *common goals*, and contribute

COMMUNICATING

1. Preparing the message

Are you quite clear how to set about providing your people with the business context of their work?

1.1 *When did you last up-date your team on the business situation?*	
	Brief references at last team meeting on 10 June
When do you next intend to do so?	
	More fully at team meeting on 20 July
1.2 *What will you be trying to achieve as a result of communicating with them?*	
	Getting them to appreciate the need for improved 'customer care'

more effectively with ideas for improvement because they have a perspective on the business need .

We are not here talking about giving individual background information on a one-to-one basis, but about *team* briefing. You are trying to get a particular message across to your team *as a group* in order to establish a common vision of what needs doing (see 'Drive' style on page 30).

It is very important to keep the *message* as short and as simple as possible and in the language of those to whom it is being addressed. Are you giving them a *corporate* message, a *unit* message or a *department* or *section* message? The more removed it is from the normal work of the group, the more careful you have to be with the language you use.

Is there a danger of your using technical jargon or corporate initials with which you are familiar, but they are not? You may be using a briefing sheet, either passed down to you or your own notes. Make sure *you* fully understand what is written down; you cannot communicate a message effectively if you don't know what it means – and don't be afraid to ask!

If the message you want to get across is difficult to explain, involved or perhaps controversial, consider the use of visual aids. You may feel it is appropriate to give them copies of your brief, or you may want to have some *key* points on a flip- or marker-board.

If you do use visual aids, remember *it is not a presentation*. There is a danger that visual aids become the sole and impersonal focal point, destroying the *personal touch* so vital to effective communications. If the information is business sensitive be very careful not to leave it lying around!

1.3	*What is the minimum message you want to get across to them?* *Write down the first draft, and then rewrite it until you are left with the essential elements in a language that they will be able to understand:* *Do you fully understand the meaning and content of what you are going to say? If not, who can you ask to clarify it?*	*Our standards of customer care are inadequate* *Demonstrate increasing customer complaints and resulting loss of business* *Jim and Jane have assembled information; two areas of uncertainty - will ask boss*
1.4	*Are you going to use any aids to help you get the message across?* *How will you use them to keep the communication informal?*	*Pre-prepared flipcharts from Jim* *I'll explain them at the start and then display on the wall*
1.5	*Are you planning to use any sensitive information?* *Consider the risks and opportunities of using it. How can you overcome the risks and exploit the opportunities?*	*Need to stress information is useful to competitors - care from them and no copies! Will make big impact*

But what about confidential information? How much should you pass on? I have found that if you trust people with sensitive information, explaining its sensitivity, they will respond responsibly; if you withhold it they will quickly find out – we have become very creative in accessing the grapevine!

2. Getting the message across

You now know *what* you are going to say, *how* and *why* you are going to say it. Try to imagine the situation in which you are going to communicate. Is it going to be at a special meeting, called to enable you to get an important message across, or will it be a small but important part of a meeting called for another purpose?

Since communicating regularly and informally is such an important part of management, it is probably most sensible to build it into your normal team meetings, as a regular agenda item. The most natural and time-efficient approach is to get together with those reporting to you approximately every two weeks, and briefing them at that meeting on the business background to the performance items you are going to be discussing.

It is important to ensure that the layout of the room encourages an informal atmosphere, both for you communicating and those being communicated to. Try to avoid a layout in which you are 'addressing the troops', separate from them, creating an 'us and them' division, particularly if the message is going to be difficult for them to accept. It is very easy for any visual aids you decide to use to lead you into a presenting mode, where you give out and they receive. Where will your visual aids be?

2. Getting the message across

Do you know how to make sure that those listening to you really understand and commit to what you are putting across?

2.1 Are you going to call a special meeting, or build the message into a regular meeting or into one already set up?	*Add to planned team meeting on customer care*
2.2 If you are intending to provide the information in a normal meeting, how will it fit into the agenda? Will its content and place on the agenda help or hinder other agenda items?	*Make it first item on 'customer care' agenda - help to show need to improve*
2.3 How are you going to lay out the room? Will your use of visual aids affect the lay-out of the room? Who will provide them?	*Usual team meeting layout* *I'll sit near flipchart and will stand to use Jim's charts*

If you have to talk to a large group – for example, if you have to communicate with two levels of the organization – try to keep the layout as circular as possible. If you sit around a table, as in a normal meeting, you will be seen to be part of the team, and members will get involved more quickly. *Refer* to your aids, if you have them, but *don't* remain standing next to them – eye contact is essential.

One key step , which never fails to relax the atmosphere, is to get a response from your 'audience' *as soon as possible*. This can be done by asking one of the group if he or she understands the points so far, or, something more open, such as 'What's you reaction to that, Jim?' Ideally one of them will ask a question early on, which will then encourage the rest.

In order to help them grasp what you have been saying, summarize the key points as you go along. Don't do what I observed one technical manager do on one occasion – he read out his brief *twice* (lifelessly on both occasions), just in case someone hadn't taken it in the first time!

You have to *observe* people listening and understanding, and you will probably have to make sure by *questioning*. You can use checking behaviour, or encourage *them* to use it, (it can be a useful sign of their interest). If you want to make sure that they have taken in what you have been saying, ask someone what he or she considers to be the key points so far !

Do remember to keep the message short and in appropriate language. The occasional smile will help them to retain their interest in you, but be careful of using jokes. They can help at the start to relax you all, but only if it suits your style, and not if you are about to announce a 're-sizing' programme!

2.4 *How will you get an early response from the group, in order to relax the atmosphere as soon as possible?*	*I'll ask for reactions to my opening on our poor customer care performance; if no response, I'll ask Brian*
2.5 *How do you intend to make sure that they have understood your message?* *Check the essential elements in Section 1.3 on page 81.* *How do intend to get them to commit to the message you will be putting across?*	*They should ask questions; checking; regular summaries* *Watch for reactions; stress everyone's involved in the problem, and show <u>my</u> commitment to improvement*
2.6 *Do you regularly communicate in this way with your team?* *If not, consider ways of making it a regular method of managing:*	*Not as a regular agenda item* *Will regularly report back on Company customer care and cost performance at future team meetings*

Perhaps the most important element of communicating, after clarity and brevity, is *commitment*. It is so easy, particularly if you are passing on someone else's message, to opt out of responsibility for what is being said -- it's what 'Management' wants to be said, (*of course I don't agree with it!*). If you demonstrate your own enthusiasm for the message you are putting across, they will very soon pick it up and not only understand but be convinced.

3. Encouraging improvement

By means of skilful questioning, checking and summarizing, you now have your team understanding the information you have given them, interested in its significance and committed to what needs doing as a result. But sharing information in this way rarely stops at this point – at least in a *dynamic team*.

The members of the team are now going to want to contribute ideas, as well as questions, to improving the situation you have been outlining for them. Two-way information flows will normally develop from data sharing to proposals for action. But do you want their ideas? Are you prepared to accept their contributions? Have you the *time* for consultation?

It is advisable to consider before the communication session takes place whether or not you and your team have the *authority* to suggest particular action. If you are uncertain, could you clarify the position with your boss, or with another manager who may be glad of your group's suggestions? If that is not possible or advisable, you should explain the situation at the start, in order to avoid frustration later. The

3. Encouraging improvement

Are you expecting communications meetings to provide you with ideas for improvement?

3.1 How likely are members of the group to want to contribute ideas on the subject you are intending to communicate to them?	*Not initially, but they will when they appreciate the Company and department situation*
3.2 How prepared are you for the meeting or agenda item to move from sharing information to developing ideas?	*I have ideas in the plan, but I want more from them*
3.3 Is it within your area of authority to encourage ideas for improvement relating to this topic? *If uncertain, could you obtain it in advance?* *If not, are you ready to explain why the discussion cannot develop in this way?*	*Depends on ideas - will clear with boss later if any doubts* *Will explain I'll be seeing boss if outside our area*

communication process very soon becomes devalued when a group realises nobody wants to act on its suggestions.

If you are willing and able to encourage them to respond and offer ideas (*MCI Unit 9.0*), remember that 'Focusing' (Chapter 2) offers you a valuable aid to joint problem-solving. However you encourage ideas, *you must listen* to what they are saying; checking what you understand each individual to be saying is the most immediate way of doing this.

Try to *build* on ideas or encourage others to do so – pairs can work very creatively if you find yourself with too many ideas to handle.   Building not only demonstrates your own commitment but will ensure the maximum commitment of the team to the action agreed as a result of the discussion.

As their proposals develop, be seen to make notes of the ideas that are agreed to be acceptable. If you have used a flip- or marker-board, write them up on the board, and so demonstrate your commitment to progressing the ideas. Don't forget that ideas on a marker-board need to be recorded by someone before being wiped clean!

If you do move from sharing information to sharing *ideas*, it is essential that you are seen to be progressing the ideas that they have given you. Take action between meetings, and do not fail to report back on progress – or get someone else to – at the next meeting. If no action has been possible or an idea has proved to be impractical, be sure to explain the reason why when you next meet.

Communicating information, then, not only ensures an informed and motivated workforce, but also provides the stimulus for everyone to contribute to the on-going process of improving performance at all levels in the organization. It is a skill well worth the investment in getting right!

3.4 *How are you going to make sure you listen to their contributions?*	
	Regular use of checking, and building on suitable ideas
3.5 *How are you going to make sure you have noted the most practical ideas for future action?*	
	Make notes initially and then ask Jim to put on flipchart
3.6 *Consider how you might progress the ideas after the meeting:*	
	Will see each individually during August. Will discuss their ideas with boss at next review meeting
Do you have a follow-up meeting planned?	
	Yes, next team meeting after holidays, 6 September

MEETING/COMMUNICATING CHECKLIST

Think of the next meeting you will be chairing which will include communicating. Use the following checklist to make sure you have considered all the key elements, by ticking boxes and summarizing your priority action (*Communicating action in italics*):

Tick the appropriate boxes:	YES	NO	ACTION REQUIRED
1. Are you clear about the purpose of the meeting?	☑	☐	☐
2. Have you fixed the date and time of the meeting?	☑	☐	☐
3. Have you decided on an agenda?	☐	☑	☑
Do you need to circulate it in advance?	☐	☑	☐
4. Is there any action agreed at the previous meeting which needs to be reviewed at this one?	☑	☐	☑
5. *Are your clear what is the key message you want get across in the communicating session?*	☑	☐	☐
6. Have you considered who are the key people who need to attend,	☑	☐	☐
and how they are likely to behave?	☐	☑	☐
7. Have you arranged a suitable location?	☑	☐	☐
8. Are you going to need any visual aids?	☑	☐	☑
other resources?	☑	☐	☐
Have you arranged for their delivery?	☐	☑	☑
9. *Have you decided on an appropriate lay-out?*	☐	☑	☐
10. *Is any of the information you are planning to discuss sensitive?*	☐	☑	☐
11. *Have you considered how you are going to get an early response from those present?*	☐	☑	☐

12. Which of the interpersonal skills are going to be most important to you in this meeting?:

INFORMING	☐	RESPONDING	☐	SUGGESTING	☐
QUESTIONING	✓	BUILDING	✓	INTERRUPTING	☐
CHECKING	✓	BRINGING IN		SUMMARIZING	✓

Tick the appropriate boxes:	YES	NO	ACTION REQUIRED?
13. *Have you considered how you are going to ensure the group's understanding*	✓	☐	☐
and commitment to your message?	☐	✓	✓
14. Have you considered how you are going to get the group to reach consensus when it is appropriate?	☐	✓	✓
15. *Are you prepared for the discussion to move on to generating ideas?*	✓	☐	☐
Are you likely to have the authority to implement them?	✓	☐	☐
16. Are there any items on the agenda for which you may need to change your personal style?	✓	☐	☐
17. Are there any items for which lack of time is likely to be a help or a hinder factor?	✓	☐	✓
18. Have you considered how you are going to record the agreed action?	✓	☐	☐
19. Have you considered how you are going to progress the agreed action after the meeting?	☐	✓	✓
20. Is this meeting likely to be an opportunity to monitor individual or group performance?	✓	☐	☐

Make a note of any priority action you now need to take: *I need examples of other departments' monthly reporting methods to include on agenda, for comparison with ours last month – I'll get Jim to prepare one flipchart urgently.*

They won't like my proposed changes. They'll be more committed – and may come up with something better – if I ask them! We only have one month to implement, so I must get agreement to any new ideas within one week.

MEETING/COMMUNICATING CHECKLIST

Think of the next meeting you will be chairing which will include communicating. Use the following checklist to make sure you have considered all the key elements, by ticking boxes and summarizing your priority action *(Communicating action in italics)*:

Tick the appropriate boxes:	YES	NO	ACTION REQUIRED
1. Are you clear about the purpose of the meeting?	☐	☐	☐
2. Have you fixed the date and time of the meeting?	☐	☐	☐
3. Have you decided on an agenda?	☐	☐	☐
Do you need to circulate it in advance?	☐	☐	☐
4. Is there any action agreed at the previous meeting which needs to be reviewed at this one?	☐	☐	☐
5. *Are your clear what is the key message you want get across in the communicating session?*	☐	☐	☐
6. Have you considered who are the key people who need to attend,	☐	☐	☐
and how they are likely to behave?	☐	☐	☐
7. Have you arranged a suitable location?	☐	☐	☐
8. Are you going to need any visual aids?	☐	☐	☐
other resources?	☐	☐	☐
Have you arranged for their delivery?	☐	☐	☐
9. *Have you decided on an appropriate lay-out?*	☐	☐	☐
10. *Is any of the information you are planning to discuss sensitive?*	☐	☐	☐
11. *Have you considered how you are going to get an early response from those present?*	☐	☐	☐

2. Which of the interpersonal skills are going to be most important to you in this meeting?:

INFORMING	☐	RESPONDING	☐	SUGGESTING	☐
QUESTIONING	☐	BUILDING	☐	INTERRUPTING	☐
CHECKING	☐	BRINGING IN	☐	SUMMARIZING	☐

Tick the appropriate boxes:	YES	NO	ACTION REQUIRED?
13. *Have you considered how you are going to ensure the group's understanding*	☐	☐	☐
and commitment to your message?	☐	☐	☐
14. Have you considered how you are going to get the group to reach consensus when it is appropriate?	☐	☐	☐
15. *Are you prepared for the discussion to move on to generating ideas?*	☐	☐	☐
Are you likely to have the authority to implement them?	☐	☐	☐
16. Are there any items on the agenda for which you may need to change your personal style?	☐	☐	☐
17. Are there any items for which lack of time is likely to be a help or a hinder factor?	☐	☐	☐
18. Have you considered how you are going to record the agreed action?	☐	☐	☐
19. Have you considered how you are going to progress the agreed action after the meeting?	☐	☐	☐
20. Is this meeting likely to be an opportunity to monitor individual or group performance?	☐	☐	☐

Make a note of any priority action you now need to take:

Communicating
links to other skills in
the Manager's Toolkit series

Each skill in this workbook not only links directly with other 'information' skills in the workbook (2 and 4), but also with other skills from the toolkit on page 13 (5, 6, 8 and 9).

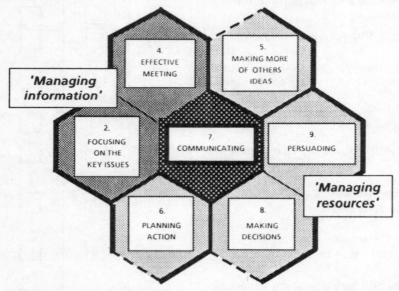

Communicating frequently involves providing the business context of a plan (6), and, as we have seen, other people's ideas (5) may be required in the course of a communicating session.

In order to make a decision (8) or to persuade other people (9), it is important that the purpose of the decision or the reason for what is being persuaded are communicated effectively to those involved.

Index

bold type denotes main references